I Was the King of Spain

Griff Griffiths

I Was the King of Spain

Olympia Publishers
London

www.olympiapublishers.com
OLYMPIA PAPERBACK EDITION

A CIP catalogue record for this title is
available from the British Library.

ISBN: 978-1-80074-795-1

This is a work of creative nonfiction. The events are portrayed to the
best of the author's memory. While all the stories in this book are
true, some names and identifying details have been changed to
protect the privacy of the people involved.

First Published in 2022

Olympia Publishers
Tallis House
2 Tallis Street
London
EC4Y 0AB

Printed in Great Britain

Dedication

To my brilliant mum and dad. Without them, none of this stuff would have happened.

Acknowledgements

To all my loyal mates, especially Magoo.

These stories are all true. They are in no particular order. Think of this book as a beautiful swimming pool in the sun, you can dive in whenever you want.

Middle son of Gypsy Witch and a West London car dealer, born into a very well-known, close-knit, large family from Notting Hill — I was a market trader, tyre fitter, professional musician, artist, entrepreneur, furniture dealer, gilder, property portfolio, professional comedian, model, sports therapist, songwriter, producer, freemason, father. Lifelong mental health sufferer, a massive breakdown left me suicidal, and in an institution, believing I was the King of Spain.

Documented are tales from emergency operation to avoid arm amputation after being hit twice by the same car, to a bizarre £25,000.00 drug deal involving armed Arabs, The Beatles photographer Bob Freeman and Led Zep front man Robert Plant in a Marrakech street market, to sexual encounters with one of Kid Creole's Coconuts after a Pet Shop Boys Hollywood party, to business dealings with the Kray brothers, to reggae band Aswad breaking up a fight with '80s heart-throb Rick Astley in the foyer of a Gibraltar hotel, to a plane load of state funded Russian football hooligans helping me find true love in Spain, to saving the life of one of the rapper duo Salt 'N' Pepa at a London Smash Hits party, to starting and selling a successful business, fooling experts in the world of antiques, to having a gap decade, then another five years off, currently drumming in a Status Quo tribute band and a The Jam tribute band.

I was banned from my youth club for eating a tadpole — the straw that broke the camel's back. Other offences included: disrupting a church service by hiding in a cupboard then bursting out during prayers, tipping an industrial waste bin into the open top of the organiser's convertible Triumph Stag and having a hand pinned by a dart to a dartboard but still winning a 50p bet.

I was in LA relaxing round the pool at the house of the producer we were going to work with in Hollywood Hills — Richard James Burgess. A couple days before studio time started, we were there, waiting to be introduced to the English engineer working with us for the twelve-to-fourteen-week period. He was flown from the UK, he arrives, and we meet him. To me he's very familiar — after a while he kind of remembers me from somewhere (not such a surprise as the music industry is very incestuous, and after drumming for decades our paths could have certainly crossed) so we go through various bands etc., studios we worked in, people we both knew, eventually we realise that we were both in the same class at primary school from the age of five till nine. He knew all my family — small world, eh? A very talented and knowledgeable sound engineer I believe now producing. Every year he's on telly loads at Xmas as he engineered "Do They Know it's Christmas" — his name is Stuart Bruce.

Boris Becker ran my wife over.

Televised Smash Hits awards live from The Albert Hall (proper rock and roll gig). After the event went to a music biz party at a film studio in London somewhere — chatting with a group, in a circle including rappers Salt-N-Pepa, out of the comer of my eye I see something falling from the ceiling and instinctively push one of the Salt-N-Pepa girls out of the way as a massive film studio light smashed to the ground exactly where she stood. I pretty much saved her life that night. Not a great deal was said, certainly no "thanks for saving my life" comments. We all kind of went "WOW" and wandered off to enjoy the party. I often wondered if she remembers that scare, and if she wonders what would have happened if I hadn't been there to save her. A twist on the classic film "It's a Wonderful Life".

I firmly believe if it wasn't for my actions that night, (which were by no means heroic, but instinctive) the Salt-N-Pepa rap duo would have become a solo act.

Went on a thirty-four date UK and Ireland tour to promote the Hitachi Super Woofer Portable stereo system — Odyssey, Edwin Star, Dollar. Two weeks after the tour ended, was wandering through West Hampstead and bumped into David Van Day who, after being with me for thirty-four nights in a row, pretended not to remember me — WANKER.

At the time he was married to Thereza Bazar. The singer in Dollar — however, Chris Quentin (the Coronation Street actor) was always with us as he was shagging her every night.

I wonder if Van Day remembers that?

When I sold my business after my divorce, I was stunned by how much the properties I worked from were worth.

Large showroom, workshops, offices plus two flats above. Sold these and with advice from my little brother, together, we bought a house in Cyprus and eight properties in East London, hoping the UK would win the Olympic bid — which we did. Immediately the properties pretty much trebled in price. My brother Gareth urged me to invest, which I did… I invested in me! Travelled extensively, enjoying life and had fifteen years off — a gap decade plus five. To this day I still think it was a wise investment; I was thirty-eight, still fit, slim, head of hair, four bed house with no mortgage, over £800,000.00 in the bank and a 34-inch waist, son's private education paid for, just survived a destructive mental breakdown, still got over a decade before Arthritis arrives and no need for reading glasses.

Being sensible with maybe a part-time job (gardening at weekends) never crossed my mind — let's HAVE FUN!

"Well, what would you do?"

Worked in the famous "Beatles Studio" Number two at Abbey Road.

Smash Hits magazine. A picture of me under the title: GRIFF'S PARTY TIPS. Answering various questions such as favourite party drink, favourite food etc. One question was 'favourite person to meet'. I always fancied Dame Diana Rigg from The New Avengers so that was my answer. I eventually met her at a birthday party thrown by actor Terence Stamp in a West End night club, however by this time I was well past my sell-by-date and she had no interest in me at all. Another dream shattered

I drove in a charity stock car race at Wimbledon stadium. My car was a Vauxhall. I painted it white with black tiger stripes, then attached a foam orange Mohican I had made, on the roof. I had a white boiler suit with similar black tiger stripes and stuck a Mohican on my head. Got through two out of three qualifying rounds and into the final. Bros both went direct into the final, both driving massive powerful American motors. I didn't win but knocked Phillip Schofield out which was filmed and shown on Going Live.

I was on a promotional tour up and down UK (personal appearances in night clubs) but the real reason was local radio, local press, local TV promotion. DJ Neil Foxy Fox. Brilliant night, excellent bloke. Next day we were booked to be guests for the whole of Foxy's Saturday morning radio show. The singer, Billy, had pulled and I ended up sleeping in the band's van in a car park... next morning there's a knock on the van window — Billy had turned up but I overslept. On air, Neil Fox put out a distress call to find a VW camper van and wake up the bloke in it because he should be on air. So this lady bangs on the door, asks if I'm Griff — the distress call was put out for me to get my arse to Radio Wyvern because I've got to read the weather report — on the road were brilliant times. I remember Foxy travelled to work on a skateboard!

I was in the Priory thinking I was a Mediterranean monarch. The woman in the room next door thought she was married to George Michael. On the other side was a woman who couldn't stop counting… I thought "I shouldn't be here 'cos I'm royalty" — this place is full of nutters.

I'm sitting there one day wearing a sombrero and drinking a glass of Sangria. Mum and dad were there. Mum's crying. Dad says, "Say something in Spanish then," to which I replied "I don't want to."

I think my dad knew!

I'm in the mile high club.

I was at a Hollywood party being thrown by the Pet Shop Boys— (no idea what for — typical rock and roll!) I had worked in the UK with Don and Dave was from the band 'Was Not Was' and found myself outside round the pool chatting with them. Next thing, one of Kid Creole's Coconuts was within touching distance, Adriana Kaegi (everything one would imagine from a Coconut but twice as magical in real life). I say hello, she says hello (honestly wondered if she had mistaken me for somebody else). I had pulled... end of night; kiss, exchange numbers and the next day at the studio as normal, she turns up. We are together from then on for the duration of my stay. A real live Coconut, I say again, a real live Coconut. One evening we were in a French restaurant in downtown LA when some geezer dressed like a French bloke was flitting in between tables, serenading each diner with French-sounding tunes on a harpsichord. He strolls up to us, we asked him to play a request, he said yes in a West Country English accent... he was French one day, the next a Spanish Gypsy. We asked if he knew Anarchy by the Pistols — next four minutes he is slowly circling our table bashing out Anarchy dressed like a Parisian peasant playing the Pistols all through the main course.

I was working in New York remixing a few tracks at a studio owned by The System at the top of a tower block in Times Square. I went out one night, and on the way back, got stuck in the lift for six hours with the keyboardist from The Cars, Gregg Hawkes, who was working with us and sax player Bob Belden. 8 grams of cocaine plus two crates of lager — Bob Beldon spent the whole time in tears but for us it was the best six hours ever.

Sitting at some traffic lights in Wallington, Surrey and suddenly a dog ran across the road attached to a Wall's ice cream sign — terrified because the dog thought the sign was chasing it, it ran over the pedestrian crossing and knocked itself out against a wall. I jumped out to help and its owner said he had tied the dog to the sign while he was shopping. Two days later, I'm in hospital having an operation on my knee, when in walks the anaesthetist and it's the bloke who tied his dog to a Wall's ice cream sign. He says, "Blimey, small world, eh?" as he puts me to sleep.

Had two ops since then — never seen him again.

On an internal flight in Germany, I had the window seat. Sat next to me was Morten Harket — frontman from the band A-ha, I fucking hate A-ha. He immediately fell asleep. When the food came, I put his tray down and the stewardess gave me my food and put his on his tray. He was still asleep; so I ate his lunch, gave the rubbish to the stewardess and when we landed, he woke up and was none the wiser.

TAKE ON ME — TAKE HIS LUNCH, MORE LIKE

I was recording in a studio near Chelsea Reach at the Fulham end of the Kings Road and went to a local pub for lunch. Standing at the bar was London gangland legend John Bindon, wearing a bright pink tracksuit. My Dad kind of knew him so we joined him at the bar. After a few hours he said he had been given the pink tracksuit by his mate Danny La Rue and would we like to meet him (obviously I said yes) and the next thing we are in his apartment near Kensington on the piss. All weekend.

At yet another show biz party (possibly San Francisco) I beat Dave Lee Roth from Van Halen at an arm-wrestling contest.

In a busy Chinese takeaway after the pub, Friday night I said to the bloke behind the counter "Can I turn your telly over?" He said yes, so I picked it up and turned it upside down. It popped and stopped working. He was shouting "I will call the police, you broke my television."

I said, "I did ask first."

I love Billy Idol — such a brilliant advert for the rock and roll lifestyle. Thought Generation X were brilliant. King Rocker, Friday's Angels, etc. — not everyone's cup of tea but definitely mine.

Working in LA, Richard James Burgess (our producer) invites us to the opening of a nightclub that had something to do with Billy Idol's girlfriend at that time. Both Idol and his girl were mates, so along I went to meet him with my best mate Dave, who was living in LA and working as a printer. Dave also had a love for all things "Idol". Met his girlfriend in the foyer who was attached to the ceiling by 30-feet lengths of elastic all night long. Milling about inside waiting to meet Billy Idol, Dave decides to shoot off to the loo. As he does, Billy Idol appears. Richard Burgess says, "Billy this is Griff." He shakes my hand and says "Hi ya, Griff." I was star-struck. My years in the music industry I'd met untold stars; from The Beach Boys to Aled Jones, but was star-struck meeting THE IDOL! All I said was "My mate Dave's in the toilet," shook his hand and he said "Oh, OK," then wandered off. Dave returns and I told him I'd just met Billy Idol. Dave says, "What did you say?" I said, "I told him you were in the toilet." Well at least I didn't lie.

I was at a bull-ring-type of arena in Spain, watching a horse gymnastic display with my dad who was co-manager of the band at the time. Around us were loads of European employees of BMG Music. Dad was keeping an eye on Lisa Stansfield at the time, so she was with us and seated next to Dad on one side and La Toya Jackson on the other. At the time the press was rumouring that Latoya and Michael Jackson were the same person as they were never seen at the same place at the same time. I think it is confirmed now that they are in fact two different people, but back then, after chatting and being so close to La Toya, I was convinced they were one and the same.

Working in 'Do Not Erase' studios (Fulham) with producer Steve Levine (Culture Club) one afternoon, was out walking to coffee shops with Levine and Boy George, we wandered into a second-hand clothes shop where I tried on a 1966 original USA leather jacket. I had no money on me so Boy George lent me the money to buy the jacket. A few years ago, I gave the jacket to my son. We decided to research the original owner and found photos of him wearing it back in the '60s. Apparently he died in the Vietnam War. We still have the jacket.

New Year's Eve — I'm appearing live on the TV show The Hitman and Her — broadcasting from THE Hammersmith Palais, West London, where funnily enough my mum and dad met in 1956! The whole family was excited; mum and dad have invited lots of uncles and aunts etc. round to celebrate New Year and watch the live interview while enjoying a glass of fizz. Backstage, drinking heavily with Bill Wyman, his fifteen-year-old wife, and his child bride's mum! All having a great time. Next thing, a voice says "Are you Strength? You're on now." I'm pushed onto the stage still holding a pint and smoking a fag, wearing ridiculous sunglasses. There's Michaela Strachan dressed as an elf, holding a microphone, firing questions at me. The whole scene going out live on national TELLY. Dad says, "He's pissed." No! Every uncle and aunt in hysterics. Obviously didn't make a great impression. Still have to smile at the clip when watching it today! Looking back to those crazy days, all I can say is I'm glad that I don't smoke any more.

Years later our sax player, Gary Barnacle, dated Michaela Strachan for ages.

Signed a major record deal with American label Arista Records. With the advance I bought a flat in South Croydon. Due to the nature of being in a band, we were away quite a lot. One weekend we were around and decided to have a 'pants-on-your-head' party. I don't wear pants — don't know where the pants came from but between twelve to fifteen pissed party people were in my flat wearing underwear on their heads and having fun. Suddenly a knock on the door. My mate Renie answers it donning pants on his head. It's the bloke who lives upstairs asking if we could turn the music down. He's pulled into the flat, someone puts a pair of pants on his head and he's locked in the bathroom. Half hour later I need to use the bathroom so had to let him out. He hands me back the pants and off he goes.

Two days later, my little brother (who is eight years younger than me) is called into his Head of Year's office where his science teacher said "Gareth, tell your brother that I enjoyed being locked in his loo wearing pants on my head, as long as it doesn't happen every weekend."

What's the chances, eh?

I have a collection of interesting stuff (interesting to me anyway); from original SS helmets to Salvation Army hats, original Space Invaders machine I got from a French nightclub, stand up Asteroids machine, Hook, Simpsons and Dr Who pinball machines, a life-sized Darth Maul, fully armoured Spartan mannequin, and loads of other pointless purchases from over the years. Included in my collection of stuff is a life-sized Dalek which stands approximately 5 feet 10 inches — had it since 2001, it comes apart in three pieces and, when slimmer, I could fit into it.

Bored one afternoon me and my mate Jones Boy put it in the back of his car and drove to the local Tesco superstore. We put it together with me inside then he wheeled me in with a shopping basket hooked over the plunger arm, up and down the aisles, while I pointed out the items I needed, by moving the Dalek's head, pointing the seeing stick at various products. Bizarrely, nobody flinched an eye. Eventually he pushed me to the checkout, we paid, then he pushed me back to the van. Not sure what I was expecting to happen, it was a great deal of effort with very little response.

I was on a promotional tour of the UK — personal appearances, local press, TV and radio, etc. In Woolworths in Kirkaldy, Scotland, doing promo single, signing. At the same time Lofty and Windsor Davis were there from the popular BBC sitcom "It Ain't Half Hot Mum" dressed in War II soldiers signing their latest single. Maybe fourteen or fifteen young girls come to see us at but no one at all turned up to receive a signed single from them. Honestly, they were pissed right off. We shared lunch then exchanged pleasantries and went our separate ways.

Years later. I'm out of the music industry and running my own furniture company with a showroom plus HQ in Carshalton Beeches, Surrey. Windsor Davies lived locally and became a very good customer buying all sorts of interior products for his house in France. Got to know him quite well and in conversation I mentioned the "signing scene" in Scotland, pretty much believing he wouldn't remember it all, however, he did! He remembered it well — even the name of my band at the time! Obviously really pissed him of. Lovely Boy.

I witnessed a wages snatch while driving my Triumph Herald convertible with the top down. It went to court. I was a witness, and the offender went to prison.

I bought the Triumph Herald off my dad's mate's wife, Kenny Burleigh. Kenny worked for my dad. Kenny was murdered on his stag night — stabbed over forty times, by a gang outside his favourite wine bar Harveys in Streatham.

The whole gang were arrested, prosecuted, spending years in prison.

Kenny's fiancée never recovered. Family and friends suffered decades of depression. One terrible scene ruined so many lives.

What price life eh! How pointless.

One night after a comedy gig in London, two blokes approach me and say would I like to appear in the video for their next record release. Had no idea who they were but said yes and took their card. This happens to any performer regularly — loads of offers — few come to anything.

Next day I called the geezer who was manager of the band Hard-Fi — got to say I didn't know fuck all about them (different generation I guess) anyway I 'Googled' them, phoned him, next thing two days filming for their video Cash Machine (got to say, brilliant track). Through that I was asked to join a modelling agency! I was chuffed. Agency called THE UGLIES. Hey ho.

Was possible new face of Birds Eye on some microwavable dinners, they had to airbrush my tattoo out but that didn't go any further and every week for approximately four months I was dressed as a farmer advertising pesticide in Farmers Weekly.

They sent me to a couple of auditions where everybody else trying to get the job looked exactly like me.

Love dogs. Got a Rottweiler at the moment. Second 'Rotty' as last was so special — my squidgy dog. Was living in Caterham, the vets, was walking distance. I had a reminder that Squidge was due for her booster jabs so booked an appointment. The day of the appointment; walked her first, so covered in shit… wandered into reception of the vets, on either side there were two or three old ladies who all seemed to have a cat in a box, strolled up to the two receptionists on the desk who asked how they could help. Realising the whole place was looking I said "My cat ain't right. I've had her for about six months now and her behaviour is odd. Can't put my finger on it, but definitely ain't normal. What can you suggest?" After a few moments, one of the receptionists said, "It's a dog."

I said, "Blimey, that makes sense, thanks for your help," and turned to walk out — got to the door and said, "Only joking."

I was a member of Club de l'Auto, one of France's most prestigious historic car clubs. Membership doesn't depend on one's knowledge of engines or restoration skills but purely on financial situation and material worth. My introduction was through my ex-wife's parents — accepted no problem. May be eight years in a row I attended their annual rally from Paris to Deauville.

One night in Paris and four nights in Deauville, Normandy — different rallies daily. One year driving a 1910 silver ghost Rolls Royce, Roi de Belge, couple of times in 2 litre Aston Martin Drophead Lagonda and a few times in 3.5 litre Lagonda. To attend the rally, one has to dress in the period attire fitting the year of the car. Once reaching Paris, the convoy of maybe thirty or forty vehicles were accompanied by four, armed French motorbike police who stayed with us in 5-star hotels for the rally duration. Drinking all day as were the police — a license to behave as you like. Ever seen an out-of-his-head French motorbike cop go over a roundabout into a ditch? Never realised how difficult it was to wear a monocle while drunk.

New York. Nightclub. Pulled some bird. Back at the hotel, decided to go over to Central Park (two thirty-ish in the morning) for a picnic. I got the hotel kitchen to make us a hamper — fizz, nibbles, etc. Stumbled across the road for a romantic picnic in the park. Don't know how far in we went, but sat and had a couple of hours together.

Couple days later the hotel concierge, who I got to know quite well, said he'd heard that I'd ventured into Central Park for a picnic. He held my hands and said "Griff, you must never ever do that again, under no circumstances." He reckoned the only reason that we returned to the hotel safely was because the night park dwellers must have thought I was an armed lunatic!

Honestly. The way he spoke and looked at me as he held both my hands, I knew I was lucky that night to return safely!

I sold my mirror designs through many antique/reproduction furniture shops and various London auction houses. On holiday in Florida — watching a greeting from Virgin boss Richard Branson from his house on Necker Island, two of my repro mirrors hung on the walls behind him. Probably bought thinking they were old. I tried to contact him but with no joy.

Every year, a football team of mates made the trip to Parkhurst Prison on the IOW to spend the weekend playing football against the inmates. I wanted to meet Reggie Kray, so I joined them. Unfortunately for the first time in nine years Reggie had moved to another prison.

I played first half in goal after a night on acid, with a lunatic whose face was covered in tattoos, growling at me from the goal post. I let in fourteen goals in twenty minutes. Their striker was a one-legged, armed robber called Laurie Mann. The pitch only had three comers and there were inter-cross wires above head height as the previous year an inmate escaped by helicopter.

They were selling us drugs. At the screws bar after the game, we were told they let certain things happen as they had the hardest and craziest inmates in the UK.

The next day at our second game, we heard the bloke growling at me wouldn't be there as that night he'd been given a terrible beating for upsetting me!

Nice gesture.

As a kid I always wanted to join the army. I was air rifle club champion at 1.77 + .22 calibre. I joined army cadets as soon as old enough and was rifle champ at .303 range Mitcham. That all changed when I met girls.

Came home pissed. Twenty-or-so chicken drumsticks on the table. I ate five or six but they tasted moody. In the morning told mum, "Those legs were shit."

She said, "They were just defrosting." No harm done.

I was in Priory with mental issues. The bloke three doors along, was a Palace fan. One night he slit his wrists and he disappeared for a few days. I got my car keys and drove to the Palace shop — bought a Palace shirt and a card, then left them on his bed saying, "Palace have few fans, one less is a travesty — don't do that again." He said that was the loveliest thing anyone had ever done. No idea what became of him.

My mate Skinny Tim used to shoot tadpoles at people from his air rifle. Best last moments of a tadpole's life being propelled at 300 miles an hour like a white-knuckle ride at a theme park, then obliterated into pulp on my knee!

Had untold photo shoots, using all top 'happening' photographers from that era such as Sheila Rock, Spencer Raul. We needed a new shoot for an album cover. The photographer we chose was Robert Freeman (iconic Beatles photographer) and after meets with Freeman, a location shoot, rather than a studio shoot was decided upon. Eventually the two top choices were a weekend (two or three day) shoot in Bournemouth or ten days in North Africa. Choosing a trip down the M3 or nearly a fortnight split between Algeria and Morocco in North Africa wasn't a difficult one. Bournemouth can fuck off. North Africa here I come.

So, ten days before flights, out in West End with stylists choosing numerous sets of expensive outfits for the shoot. At the airport the place was empty apart from my band, Robert Freeman's girl called Mishi (makeup artist) and two other passengers we met in the VIP departure lounge as they were mates of Freeman. Robert Plant, Led Zep front man, and his fourteen-year-old son. Our manager, Alan Bown, was a mate of Robert Plant so we were introduced to him and enjoyed vpre-flight drinks together. Lovely bloke. First hotel was called La Mamounia in Marrakesh — at the time, one of the top seven hotels in the world. Planty also staying there so that night on the piss together.

Freeman & Plant decided to score some hash, each enough for a few days, so next day half-pissed in a Marrakesh street-market, they put out the feelers asking a few market traders (in very pigeon French) where they can score £25.00 each of hash. It didn't take long and we were guided away from the main streets through tiny alleyways to a house full of dodgy, scar-faced, armed Arabs. All of whom seemed to have gold teeth. This was just like a scene from an Indiana Jones movie. Anyway, garbled French was spoken and we all sit down to sample the hash. I was off my tits. The two Roberts said yes, they want it and about eight brick-sized blocks appear. Immediately the atmosphere changed, no more smiles, weapons cocked. Planty turns to me and says, "Griff, I think we've fucked up here,". We wanted £25.00 worth each, they thought we wanted £25,000.00 each.

Eventually, after what seemed like five days of shouting, everybody laughed. They shook our hands, took a picture of Planty looking terrified and off they went. Thankfully they found it funny.

During the ten days of travelling, Rob Plant was staying at nearly all the same places as us, so we became mates!

Four maybe five years later, I'm out of the music biz working hard on my furniture company. I'm in Barnes delivering an overmantel mirror to one of my customers in Barnes high street, when I hear, "GRIFF." I turn round and it's Rob Plant. He said, "What are you doing?" I said I make mirrors now and he said, "Wow that's different from drumming. I hope all goes well, take care." To this day I can't believe that he shouted and remembered me! I suppose enduring a near-death experience while being held at gunpoint in North Africa by armed drug dealers, kind of sticks in the memory.

Fan Club image Taken
in the Sahara

80's promo
shot

PARTY TIPS

GRIFF from STRENGTH

Ideal venue: My house.
Best party: The wedding reception of my friend who used to play keyboards in The Alarm.
Worst party: My gran's at Christmas.
Fave drink: Earl Grey tea — but you can't drink that at parties so I'll say tequila.
Fave cocktail: Tequila sunrise I suppose.
Fave party food: Crabsticks
Precautions before a house party: Make sure your parents are out.
Most invitable person: Jason Ball from The New Avengers
Least invitable person: it's Ashley
Fancy dress outfit: I'd go as the Barb
and

MY GUY
MAGAZINE

The 'GRAND HALL' in Ramacre

STAG & HOUNDS sign, liberated from demolition and displayed on my
shed

A 'ROCOCCO'
Gilt Framed mirror
Designed and crafted
by myself

Some of my collection of arcade machines

Signing "2 FAT DJ's" to my record label, 1984

'T' Shirts made to promote single release inspired by FRANKIE SAYS
RELAX

BRICKING IT **Four of the competing ten finalists battling it out for New Act of the Year at the Hackney Empire — hosted by Arthur Smith.** See Sa

Good Mates till this day - with comedians, Papa CJ, Henning When and Gareth Berliner, SUNDAY TIMES Magazine 2004

ONE OF MY FAVOURITES
(THE HANDS PAINTED BY MY DAD)

Comic's Choice Comedy

Griff Griffiths (*pictured*) says his mother was the seventh daughter of a seventh daughter of a Romany gypsy family. 'That means she's a witch.' He believes his father to be the seventh son of the seventh son of one of the Seven Dwarfs. Griffiths became a drummer and made his first record at the age of 14. He subsequently landed several major recording deals. He worked as a market trader. He started his own furniture company. 'And I went mad. I was in a nut house. I believed that I was the King of Spain.' Now he's a comedian. Earlier this year he was a finalist in the Hackney Empire New Act of the Year competition. You can catch his super-energetic act at Comedy Candy (Thur), Upstairs at the Queen's Head (Fri), Bath House Comedy Club (Sat) and the Comedy Pit (Mon). Here's his selection from the current London shows.

Pear-Shaped in Fitzrovia
Wed 8 & 15
'Brian Damage and Krysstal are unique and unforgettable. Jimbo also has moments of genius. A hot sweaty room where the acts on stage outnumber the amount of pints you can drink.'

Chertsey Comedy Club
Wed 15
'Great club. There's a picture of me on the wall and it's not a "Wanted"

poster! I had two standing ovations here. Look out for Nik Coppin. Get here early as it's always busy.'

Upstairs at the Queen's Head *Fri & Sat*
'Hosted by Mike Manera and Phil Klein. Always packed. Always a great night. Does Mike Manera cut Phil Klein's hair? Does Phil Klein design Mike Manera's clothes? Go along and ask Dizzy High. Or ask me – I'm here on Friday.'

Theatre Royal Comedy Night *Mon*
'Great venue, free entry, brilliant acts. No Monday blues allowed – here it's still the weekend.'

'Keep your eye out for any gig compered by Dave Ward or Nigel Numas. Pay to see Dave Dynamite and Josh Howie, the Jewish Woody Allen.'

TIME OUT MAGAZINE, 2005

Wearing "Carpet"
on my head

The same carpet
Worn as a beard -
Nearly started a
"Jihad"

With my "Market Trading" Partner John McKay
Dressed in period clothing
Portobello Road

The finalists line up for the judges at
"THE MADHAT PARTY"

"HARLEQUIN"
style mirror and
table set

"MOD" battle of Hastings

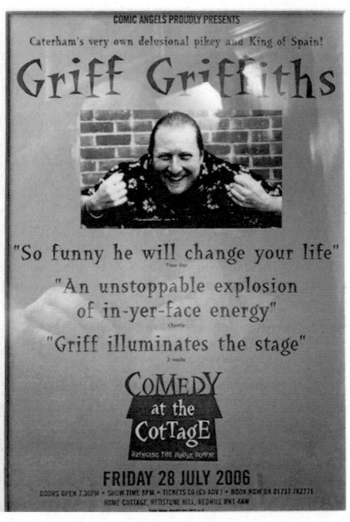

Has to keep this promotional poster. The quotes are taken from "TIME OUT" magazine.

"SO FUNNY IT WILL CHANGE YOUR LIFE"

No Pressure then!!

A couple of miles away from my house, a beautiful Victorian school was being demolished to make way for shit flats. I broke in one evening and took all the toilet seats out, cleaned them up, put mirrors in them and sold the lot.

Don't class that as theft as they were going in the skip.

Every second show on daytime television now seems to be a programme where some privately educated hat-wearing tart sneaks around the cleanest council tip in England "rescuing" some deceased grandmother's war era wardrobe to paint yellow and sell for enormous profit.

I was ahead of my time.

The guitarist in one of my bands was Mickey Hutton; author, TV presenter, professional comedian and actor. He was big pals with Jimmy Bradford (Nail) from Auf Wiedersehen, Pet. At the height of the show's popularity, we went pub crawling around Covent Garden with Nail and Michael Elphick, dancing on tables in the Cheddar Cheese pub.

In LA recording an album, staying in a hotel/apartment just along from the Chinese Theatre. Hollywood, four bed apartment, living upstairs is British actor Roy Dotrice and his wife. He was always busy appearing in American television shows (father of Michelle Dotrice — Betty from Some Mothers Do 'Ave 'Em). First few weeks got on fine (he was the mate of our manager Alan Bown) and through him we got invited to Rod Stewart's birthday party. However, eventually he came to hate us and our rock and roll partying antics.

One night had a party food fight; music, furniture broken, girls etc. He called the hotel manager who called the record company in the UK, who contacted the studio in LA, and they pulled the plug on our sessions. Studio over, hotel cancelled so stayed there three or four weeks with a mate. Ha!

The record company gave us a second chance, sent us to New York where we pretty much did the same thing. Thought I was an indestructible rock star. History proves I wasn't.

I walked into a restaurant on the Island of Rhodes, Ex-President of The United States, George Bush Senior was having lunch surrounded by security. I asked to meet him and the ex-president motioned me over to join him. I sat, had a glass of wine, and shared his salad.

November 1992. A fire broke out at Windsor Castle. I was dealing with many top-end interior designers at the time through my furniture company. One of these contacted me to design and make twelve large gilt mirrors for the ball room at Windsor Castle. My mum was over the moon working hard trying to get "by appointment to her Majesty the Queen" on all our stationery. However, it wasn't Windsor Castle… it turned out to be THE CASTLE HOTEL, WINDSOR.

I loved to box (never any good but was very fit and loved it). I was pissed at Epsom Derby Day and decided to fight for money with some Gypsies. So, sun blazing, pissed, shirt off, ring of betting onlookers. One punch and I'm on the deck! Won't be doing that again.

Early punks wore school blazers. I went to Toyah Wilcox's party wearing mine, because I was still at school. Met Adam Ant for the first time. Toyah at that point was sleeping in a coffin.

Shopping in Tesco's, Caterham, a short walk from where I lived at the time. I found some house keys and handed them to customer services saying that someone will be looking for those later... walked home and realised the keys were mine.

As a musician I was featured with photos in: Smash Hits, My Guy, Blue Jeans, Just Seventeen… to name just a few.

I went out with a girl whose dad invented the gripper rod — a unique device sold globally that attaches carpet to the floor. Every time a length is sold anywhere in the world, she gets a percentage. She's minted. I said to my dad "Why can't you invent something?"

He said, "I did, I invented you."

I had twenty-six holidays in one year.

I was sponsored by the drum company TAMA. They would send me all the new TAMA products free, as well as drumsticks, etc. I had to mention TAMA in interviews and the TAMA logo was visible in videos.

I stopped playing drums for nearly thirty years — my family and building a business took over. I eventually sold everything music related, including six or seven TAMA kits.

I had my own fan club.

1991 David Icke was all over the TV and press with his bizarre thoughts. On one of our Croydon geezers' trips to play football against Parkhurst Prison inmates. We decided to have a "disciples of Icke" trip. He lived just outside Ryde on the IOW.

T-shirts printed, and en masse, we gather outside his house with finger bells and plastic trumpets. One of the lads contacted local press and a couple of journalists and a photographer met us in the pub so they could cover it. Obviously, it didn't take them long to realise we were out for a laugh, but they still joined us on the uphill walk to Icke's house... he wasn't in!

I was a member of The Veteran Car Club of Great Britain and attended many rallies throughout the UK and Europe. For ten years in a row, I drove in the famous London to Brighton Run — twice in a 1903 De Dion Bouton, other times in 1902 Panhard Levassor (a French taxi) which had original bodywork and is now in a museum in Holland.

My son has been on the London to Brighton Rally over twenty times.

I bought two old Victorian school desks to sell in my shop. A good customer of mine, whose kids' nursery ceiling I had painted like a cloudy sky, was emigrating to New Zealand, he was a motorbike traffic policeman. He wanders in and says, "Blimey, that's exactly the same as my old school desk." Unbelievably, after closer inspection, he found his name written inside and it was his old school desk from thirty years previous. He obviously bought it and had it shipped to New Zealand when he left. Now, what's the chances of that!

Crystal Palace were in the Cup Final at Wembley. I had the idea of every Palace fan singing Beatles songs in unison. So, I bought twenty Beatles wigs off Amazon. They were £3.00 reduced to £2.50 each and were the worst Beatles wigs in the world. In hindsight I should have spent an extra couple of quid as when I put mine on, I looked like a fat Ernie and Bert from Sesame Street. A wig made my mate Pat Towers, looks like Peter Beardsley and another mate, JT, looked like a fat Pam Ayres. I kind of realised it was a ridiculous idea when I found two discarded Beatles wigs on the platform at Victoria Station on the way home.

Looking back, do I think it was a ridiculous idea? "Yeah, yeah, yeah!"

I knew this girl called Tammy — very sexy, always fancied her (she got her tits out a couple of times as a page three model). Hadn't seen her for years. Was at this party in Southwark and there she was. After what I remember being bloody hard work, I eventually got her to come to my house. Both were worse for wear, me realising there's no way I'm getting her into bed — I can deal with that. Hours of heart-to-heart conversation and she's saying she wants to end it all; she's had enough, life is taking its toll, she's been seriously thinking about suicide. I say, "So have I, let's end it together." I run upstairs and return with a forty-five revolver, starter pistol. I lay it on the table and say, "If you're serious, I'm serious too. I'll go first. I'll see you on the other side." I put it in my mouth and pulled the trigger. BANG. I fall face first down on to the floor. Tammy screamed for at least a half hour. What was I thinking?

Called her a cab and never saw her again. Some women have no sense of humour.

Used to go rabbiting — put ferret down warren, cover as many holes with nets, rabbits scarper, and some are caught by nets. Years ago, we sold them all to butchers. Approximately 90% had myxomatosis so weren't edible. The disease makes their eyes stick together (bit like conjunctivitis). Decades later, I'm now fifty-eight and I find it rather cruel. Strangely I've never eaten rabbit.

Working in New York, I stayed in Mayflower Hotel. I was in the hotel bar in New York and our Manager, Alan Bown, spots Jo Cocker, one of his old mates. He called us over, Cyndi Lauper turns up and we spend the whole night on the piss with them.

Gate-crashed the wedding of Pink Floyd's Dave Gilmour's daughter in Lindos, Greece by dressing all in white and wearing a false mohican and sunglasses. The two cordons of security let me through as I looked so bizarre.

I think she married one of the members of Razorlight.

I Was at an event at Epsom Racecourse celebrating Derby Day, just a few days before my wedding. It was hosted by Samsung. Myself and my future wife were on the top deck of an open-top bus when two or three suited security men, accompanied by an interpreter, walked up followed by a tiny well-dressed Korean bloke carrying a cake (which was bigger than him) saying 'Good Luck GRIFF & DEB' written across it. Through his translator he said he wished us decades of happiness.

Turns out he was the CEO of Samsung. My first thought was WOW! My second was that; two years previous on Derby Day I was out of my head, bare-knuckle boxing Gypsies only yards away. Both excellent memories and both with the same outcome — neither my boxing career nor marriage lasted the distance.

Every year I would attend the Henley Regatta, always enjoying the facilities of the world-famous Remenham Rowing Club as my ex-wife's dad was a member. Without my relationship with his daughter there is no way on God's clean earth I would ever be accepted. You can dress expensively in the Henley Regatta attire: blazer, white slacks, brogues, a Remenham Rowing Club tie with matching silk handkerchief and straw boater hat, yet those river-based posh fuckers can tell at a glance I ain't one of them.

Reckon taking my shirt off and sticking a lit fag in the life-sized Remenham Rowing Club stuffed bear raffle prize blew my cover.

I had a successful venture selling secondhand clothes, way ahead of anybody else. Started with a market stall at a local Friday flea market and eventually having stalls at Camden Lock, Greenwich and Portabello Road markets. We'd buy stuff from charity or second-hand clothes shops for literally pennies and sell for £20.00 or £30.00. Main source was jumble sales. Ten Grandad shirts for 50p — each one sold for £10.00 or £15.00. Nobody else did it at that time. Before the "period clothing boom" a suit bought from a charity shop was no more than 30p.

With my pals Ian the Mod and John McKay, we would dress in outfits we sold — Fedora hats, old brogues, three-piece suits. We had one or maybe two years of wonderful, profitable times. During this period, no idea how, but we decided to have a night out in London dressed in stuff we sold as 1930 and 1940's gangsters: suits, big overcoats, hats, two or three violin cases. Turnout was good — maybe twenty-five of us in all. Train to Victoria, tube to Covent Garden, pub crawl... great fun, no aggro. Our attire was appreciated by everyone. Charing Cross underground on the way home, getting tickets etc. across the vestibule a group of twenty to twenty-five black dudes. By the way they behaved it was clear they wanted trouble. It ended up with us lot in crescent- shape facing them, maybe 12′ away, also in similar formation. I'm in front, facing some massive track-suited leader. I said, "After three I'm gonna chin this cunt, then you lot, steam in." He was in front of me swaying about, staring at me. One, two, three, I hit that cunt so hard he came off his feet. All hell breaks loose. Don't recall much till me and Jones Boy were bashing these two blokes on a stairway. Grabbed from behind and a police helmet falls to the floor — two policemen manhandle me away into the back of a van outside station. I was saying they started it, we wanted to get away. Bang, doors slam behind me. I'm nicked. twenty-five minutes later, doors open, mates are there, coppers say, "Go on, fuck off.' So I did. They came unstuck. Bullies, starting a fight with those they thought were weak. I hate bullies. That occurred late 1980s. All blokes on both sides received some kind of visible wound the next day. To this day, my pals recall that row with an amount of pleasure, as I'm sure our opposition that night remembers it. Today people would lose their lives in such a fight.

Going to a party in Notting Hill, West London, popped in pub first, then in cab on the way to the party. I got in front, two friends in the back speaking with cabbie, he tells me before driving for a living he was a pro footballer. He played for Brentford. I told him my uncle Ron Peplow played pro football for Brentford. He said he was in the same team and knew him well — he knew Ron's wife, Rene, (my auntie) he said he went out with her sister for a while — June. I said, "That's my mum!" Got to the party and phoned dad, told him the story, he knew the bloke. I said he could have been my dad, to which he replied "If he was your dad, you wouldn't be you."

I can only imagine the groupie attention proper rock stars receive. Being in a band seems to impress girls... even in a band with limited success, such as the bands I've been in. One memorable scene, (definitely in UK) my singer and I were in some hotel room (as was usual when we were away), he'd pulled, so I stay clear for hour or so. Then decide it's time for bed... open room door and she's naked in my bed, covered in baby oil saying our singer can't fulfil her and she wants me. I'm in no mood, got busy day next day with an early start. She won't go and ain't taking no for an answer. I throw all her clothes out the window, maybe four or five floors up, call security and kick her out naked into the corridor. At this exact moment, as a single fifty-eight-year-old, I would stick an angry wasp up my arse to be in such a situation. What the fuck was I thinking!

My dad was a boxing champion in the army while serving with the Royal Electrical Mechanical Engineers.

The writer John Sullivan wrote Only Fools and Horses in the offices above my shop before I bought the premises. It already was a fertile breeding ground for excellent ideas.

My unique mirror and furniture creations were featured in
many interior design magazines:

The World of Interiors

House & Garden

Homeflair (front cover feature)

Period Living

House & Home

To mention but a few

Creating a successful business eventually took its toll — ended up working seven days a week. Would have mates round but would never see them as I would be working. I had money but I was depressed.

One Saturday, my manager wasn't in. I sent the two Saturday kids home, sat facing the door in what, at the time, I thought was a "throne". As customers came in, anything they liked I gave it to them free. Didn't take long till shop keepers on my parade became aware of what I was doing. These were local business owners who I'd known for seven or eight years. Rather than coming in and trying to help, nearly all of them contacted friends telling them I was giving stuff away. Two couples were taking out an 8 feet x 4 feet table plus twelve chairs when a mate of mine, Aaron, visited, saying "Wow, you OK?" Told him I gave the table as a gift. He told them to fuck off, put the stuff back, can't they see I'm confused. After, he locked the door. The start of my bizarre journey as THE KING OF SPAIN.

To this day, twenty years later, can't believe those local shopkeepers behaved that way.

Mum and dad went to Florida and on their return, they gave us three boys American-style presents. Both my brothers received US style clothing: baseball caps, college-style jackets. I got a silver identity bracelet with GRIFF engraved on the front, my house phone number on the back (similar to what's attached to my Rottweiler's collar) — info in case I get lost. Hey ho. I wore it loads.

One night, walking home off our tits, me and my mate 'Chip Shop' jumped a wall into the grounds of a private boys' school maybe half mile from my house. We smashed up the beds of flowers and destroyed the 10-foot pampas grass.

Next morning, there's a telephone call asking for GRIFF. It was the school caretaker who found my ID bracelet among the remains of his cherished pampas grass. Got my mum to go and get it.

If two wankers got into my garden and started destroying stuff, they'd get a 7-inch crossbow bolt in the face.

Been ejected from Crystal Palace football home and away games at least ten times. Brighton away game (massive rivals of Palace), the Brighton fans were throwing potatoes with razor blades sticking out of them at us.

2004, my first year of comedy — I was a finalist in all of the respected national comedy competitions: So You Think You're Funny?
Amused Moose Comedy's Hot Starlets
Hackney Empire
Laughing Horse
The London Comedy Festival
Spent three years consecutively appearing at shows in Edinburgh Fringe.

One of my shoes, after more than four decades, is still on top of the roof of Parkhurst Prison.

Don't want to dwell on mental issues really as I truly believe too many "sufferers" are "milking it". Let's hope I'm mistaken about that. I've suffered mental health issues forever. Wanted to end it — drove to Bristol to jump off Clifton Suspension Bridge. At the time I arrived the tide was out, revealing a disgusting rubbish-filled wasteland. I decided not to jump because I didn't want to enter the afterlife covered in shit.

Question on social media: "Who's the most famous person you ever met?" My answer… "I played chess with **GOD.** He was on the same ward as me when I was "The King of Spain". Trump that, you cunts!

I was arrested for stealing a Manchester United away colours scarf in Alders sports department.

I ate a two meal sized tin of dog food ensuring I won an eating competition.

After I sold my business, I learnt to fly and sail.

My little brother is a very successful businessman — he is a lifelong member of the MCC.

I got twenty t-shirts printed, thinking maybe my mates would wear them in the pub on a Friday. 'GEEZERS 4 JESUS' — waste of fucking money.

If that had been received with a bit more positivity, I thought the 'Wives and Girlfriends' would have worn 'LADIES AGAINST HADES'.

However, in these troubled times wearing a shirt displaying that logo could result in a beheading.

Signed quite a few record contracts during my time as a professional drummer. The biggest was an album deal with American label Arista. Released quite a few singles, unfortunately didn't sell enough so album never came out. After two and a half years we were dropped. Sometime later, a bill arrived (which I still have) stating I owe them £345,000.00. A massive amount now, enormous back in 1983. At the bottom of the bill in a box saying, "Amount to repay: NIL"!

Love sailing. I qualified as a day skipper, although the sailing fraternity I think are a bunch of fake wankers.

I have a lifetime ban from The Chichester Yacht club for misbehaving — a ban I'm very proud of.

Love WWII history. Especially Operation Overlord, the D-day Landings. I have made almost a yearly pilgrimage to visit the Normandy invasion sites for the last twenty years. Fascinated by the scale of the task undertaken, especially the attack on Pegasus Bridge — Operation Deadstick, by 2nd Battalion, Oxford and Buckinghamshire (Ox and Bucks) Light Infantry and the airborne operation to silence the guns at Merville Battery by 6th Airborne Division led by Lieutenant Colonel Terence Otway was especially heroic.

I was walking in Banstead, Surrey and sitting outside a cafe was the man himself — Terence Otway. I had to shake his hand, saying he was a true hero, to which he answered "Are you barmy?" I wandered off, followed by who I thought was his daughter (but turned out to be his young wife), who said I'd made his day! A hero from a different generation.

My grandad once told me when I was maybe five years old that dogs can speak, they just don't want to. You can't prove that; as soon as you quickly push the door open to a room where dogs are, they just stare at you. To this day, if I see two dogs sniffing each other's arses I'm sure they are talking about me.

The London gangster 'Nosher' Powell worked on the door of a Spiel owned by my dad. Many years later he worked at a nightclub in Streatham. I was there one night talking to him when a loud gunshot was heard and saw a bloke fall to the floor. The place emptied immediately! The club was renamed 'BANG' after that. Nosher's son, Gary Powell, was a friend of mine and was stunt co-ordinator in many Hollywood films: Braveheart, Snatch, Titanic. Setting himself on fire was a specialty. He invited me over to watch the opening scene of Saving Private Ryan being filmed in Ireland but stupidly I didn't go. He now lives in LA full time and is executive stunt co-ordinator on all the Bond films. Married to Laura Croft's stunt double. He dislikes enclosed spaces, open spaces, crowds, parties and conversations.

He loves Scalextric.

GOOD ON YOU MATE.

Worked with Sid James ("Carry On" star's) son — Steve James — he produced a single of mine.

My highest midweek chart position in the UK was number thirty-six — dropped outside top fifty at the end of the week. If it had remained inside top fifty at the end of the week, my drumming career would have taken a totally different route... though I would probably be dead.

I was number two in Icelandic charts.

My mum stabbed my Rottweiler when trying to break up a fight between all our dogs while cutting meat for Sunday roast — five stitches. Can't be many grandmothers who've sliced up a guard dog.

I paid £1,500.00 so my son Sam could go on a school geography field trip for ten days to Morocco... turned out he didn't even study geography and spent the whole time sitting around the swimming pool catching a tan. Well done, Sam!

West End nightclub, off my tits. Night ended and found myself outside. It was pissing down. A girl was waiting for a cab, I offered her my coat, which she put on. I thought 'what a gentleman I am'. She jumped into the cab and I never saw her again. It had my phone, wallet, house keys in it.

Still think what a gentleman I am.

Met the Queen with mum and brother when she was on walkabout in Wandsworth 1977. Met Camilla and Prince Charles, covered in shit while mountain biking in Cornwall. Met Prince on a few occasions.

I saw a UFO over Wandsworth Gas Works.

Aged fourteen to fifteen, I was a "punk". Bleached Billy Idol hair, standing at bus stop with twenty-five or so "punk" mates. No one older than sixteen — girls as well. Three cars stop opposite and five to ten MEN get out, slowly cross the road, walked straight to me. I heard "Ah, Punky." THEN I GOT KNOCKED OUT. Smashed head and slipped down bus stop. When I came round, they had beaten everybody up, even some poor businessman in a suit who was innocently waiting for a bus. He said "What the hell is going on?" Hilarious — no harm done.

Andy Taylor, guitarist with Duran Duran, has a bar in WHITLEY bay. Outside Newcastle. On the coast — RIO. I went to the opening night party.

Define the word 'gangster'? I know a lot of faces that could possibly fall into that category, without exception, none of them have the romantic well-dressed swagger and presence conjured up by the media — violent, vicious, terrifying, and to be kept at a distance.

Don't know how (as it definitely wasn't planned) but I end up in the West End, out of my tits on an 'E', with the very individuals I've just suggested to be kept at a distance. Wandering through an underpass, somewhere near Oxford Circus, walking towards us, a group of gangster-looking black blokes. I say "We gonna get mugged here." All five of them produce various knives, saying, "Don't worry, Griff, you're in safe company." The black dudes immediately fuck off. Ended up having a ball that night. A few days later, three or four phone calls inviting me out, all of which I declined. Not really my cup of tea, unless necessary, Your Honour.

Hot summer of '76, I caught grass snakes, slow worms and one adder. Took them to a pet shop in Surrey Street, Croydon, who bought them.

Back then, pick up a bit of old wood or plastic and "BINGO", there was always something hiding there. Not seen anything like that for decades.

I was going through a difficult, confused period. I came across a tiny white pill in my mum and dad's biscuit tin, one of those pills that the biscuit manufacturers put in the top of the packet to keep the biscuits fresh, I was convinced it was an Ecstasy tablet and there was a conspiracy trying to implicate my dad in the importing of class A drugs. So after a terrified rant at my parents, I put the pill in a cereal bowl and drove off to Croydon police station. There were loads of people sitting around in the waiting room. I walked to the officer on the desk and said "I found this in my dad's biscuit tin. I want you to analyse it to confirm if it's class A drugs." He looked at me like I was insane, told me to sit and wait, which I did.

Everyone was staring. I sat down holding the bowl containing the pill — began to realise how totally insane I looked, so after a few minutes I went home.

John Nichols, my mate Andy's Dad, is ninety-five. The term 'legend' seems to be used too often nowadays, one can be classed as a legend for successfully getting off paying a parking fine.

John Nichols is a true legend; a D-day veteran, serving on HMS Argonaut that duelled with German gun battery, along with French ship Le Georges Leygues, situated at Le Chaos Longues sur mer, D-day morning. If the guns were not silenced, they would shell the landing beaches, resulting in terrible loss. One of the Argonaut shells entered directly into the aperture of one gun and devastated the others.

After D-day he served in the Pacific and Mediterranean — aged only eighteen. Two years ago, on the seventy-fifth anniversary of D-Day, the French government and people decided to award all surviving D-day veterans with Croix de Guerre — the highest award possible to thank the ageing servicemen for their part in liberating their homeland. The ceremony was held on HMS Belfast — French Foreign Minister, Admirals, Foreign Legion, loads of top brass, the UK minister for defence with two bodyguards. It was in every paper and all over TV. A very proud moment and one in which it was an honour to attend.

On deck I ask one of the suited guards if he was "packing" (carrying a gun)? He winked, opened his jacket and revealed a firearm. Anyway, three days later, I'm wearing an orange apron with a name tag, working on the paint desk at B&Q Sutton — first and only time I was employed (I'd always been self-employed, and let me tell you it will be the fucking last time) this geezer walks up asking me to mix some paint — he didn't recognise me, I recognised him — it's the armed policeman from HMS Belfast. I sort his paint and ask "You packing today or off duty? You showed me your gun three days ago." He suddenly remembered me, then walks off to the checkout.

Two weeks previous I mixed some outside wood paint for the shed of the copper who nicked the Stephen Lawrence murderers. Detective Chief Inspector Clive Driscoll. He said "How did you recognise me?" I said because he looked very similar to my grandad — kind of Arthur Mullard-ish.

Only ever had one proper job, aged fifty-six, mixing paint in B&Q, Sutton — beyond reason how poorly that place was run.

Not sharing my experience — leave it to individual imagination — though I will say I won't be filling the Customer Care position.

In Saas-Fee, Switzerland, high in the Alps — cars left in car park, lower than the town — only pedestrians or tiny electric golf buggy things allowed. I've been there many, many times. First wife was a chalet girl there, brother-in- law runs a bar — familiar with all the restaurants, night clubs, hotel and bar owners (class them as friends). Nearing the end of season, two carloads drive non-stop to celebrate my brother-in-law's birthday, a surprise. Great times — in one bar, twenty or thirty Eastern European labourers there, arrive to do all building work in town during closed ski season. They are lairy and pissed, on our case, want a fight. We leave. They follow us to the next bar, we leave again, they follow. Outside on the street they surround me and my mate (my mate who stopped people stealing in my shop — he was once Mr Junior UK). This massive Eastern European beast has Aaron around the throat, two or three more moving in. I get a punch in first — I am not having this. Wallop, bloke seems to rise 8 feet in the air. Bash two others, then they run and I chase them with other mates. Totally justified. When I return, the beast isn't moving — he's on the deck; blood coming from ear, mouth, nose. I've probably broken his jaw. I'm writing this, my heart is racing. I think I've killed him. Back at the hotel I phone dad who tells me to get out of the country. Immediately we make our way to the lower carpark where, what we thought were police, but only traffic wardens. I hid in back of Range Rover till we're over the French border. Have nightmares to this day.

Bullies... I'm a big bloke. Honestly, why the fuck would anyone pick a fight with me when there's loads of smaller blokes roaming around?

After my drumming career ended, myself and mum and dad started a framing company. A business that eventually employed ten staff, had two full-time sales rep's; one in the North of England and one in the South. A very profitable, unique and successful venture — started by an excellent idea, the seed sown in the brilliant brain of my dad. Never set out to fool or con people but we were experts in making new stuff look old. There are many stories of selling to 'antique' dealers. My favourite is Sotheby's. I'd finished two gilt frames, washed them with a Verdigris base (Verdigris is a greenish-blue substance that forms on the metals copper, brass, and bronze after they have been left in wet or damp conditions), took them to Sotheby's, not really sure what to expect, and immediately the 'antique frame' expert arrives. I tell him a mate pulled them from a wreck of a galleon in The Solent. He confirms they are two or three hundred years old and prices them at £700.00 each (£1,400.00 the pair) and then adds them to the next auction. They appear in the Sotheby's brochure and sell for over £2,000.00. Two weeks later I wander in with another two. NEVER TRUST AN EXPERT.

Early, early days selling frames... I'm driving an old Ford Fiesta (no van). I would make five to six items, then travel around London to sell them — total cold calling.

One afternoon I sold everything I had, drove to Dad's HQ in Wandsworth. I loved that place — loads of coming and going — moody mates of Dad's. His 'Rolls' outside, my uncle Ron's Bentley directly behind it. That place buzzed. It was like walking into a scene from 'Minder'. Dad's mate Dave (who was a partner of his in Picture Gallery, three doors away) was there. His pal Alan, whose real name was never known, suffered from permanent headaches and looked exactly like a Cyber man from Dr Who. After the Richardson's were nicked, Alan went away to sea for five years. Barry the Pole, Pete the Turk, Gallant, Mickie Clark, Scots Jim, my uncle John and auntie Daphne in the office and Peter the Poof (who always arrived on a Honda Goldwing). Anyway, I walk in one day, one of the fellas had a beautiful Whole Hunter gold watch and chain for sale. I'd never seen anything like it. He says, "I've got a bit of "Tom", yours kid, for £600.00." I had exactly £600.00 on me so the watch became mine. That summer, I'm at the London Business School event, Regents Park. I went every year as a mate's wife worked there. Dinner suits, live bands, funfair rides, casino, magicians. Brilliant night out. Standing at the edge of the bumper cars, waiting for my turn... car hits the wall right in front of me. The whole ceiling of the arena crashes down, trapping my arm — I was saved from crushing by the watch. The glass broke but the watch still works.

Haven't replaced the glass as the watch still works. Always wear it when in dinner suit. Rough estimate of its value is £4,000.00.

1981 — The Bad Actors are no longer signed to record label Plastic Speech, however, our first single 'Are they Hostile' was very well received.

Decided to release a single on our own label, very punk — recorded 'Strange Love' at Spaceward Studios, Cambridge. As a band we funded its release. Record company HQ, my parent's house. John Peel plays, radio Caroline, radio Luxembourg, etc. Took an advert in NME featuring the cover — an image created by an artist mate of my dad, bound and bondage, lingerie-clad female, strapped to a post in a loft wearing high heels — the ad. Worked, we sold loads but caused an unexpected backlash from all sorts of women's lib groups.

Hundreds of damning letters and visits three to four times a day from outraged women's societies. Two girls travelled to my house in South Croydon from just outside Glasgow, on a bus, to tell me I was a disgusting sexist. NME and various publications covered the story for a couple of weeks, then some other pointless complaint took its place. However, within a month, Pamela Stevenson (wife of comedian Billy Connolly) released a record with an identical image which was produced as a forty-five cover, featuring Pamela Stevenson, dressed in lingerie, bondage, wearing heels, tied to a post in a loft — obviously inspired by our cover (stolen). Three or four days of women activists accusing us of being in a conspiracy with Pamela Stevenson. I've never met her, never heard the single — neither her track nor ours was a hit.

How sad is my life that forty years later I have led so boring and dull an existence, that such an unimportant, uninteresting, shit story manages to make it into top fifty things that happened to me? Blimey my eulogy's going to be shit.

PROOF THAT IT ACTUALLY HAPPENED

ON THE 5th DAY GOD CREATED PUNK

| ame | Ian Griffiths | Form | 1A3 | | |
| bject | Music / Drama | Set | | | |

An enthusiastic worker who suffers occasionly from silly behaviour.

J Rees Signed *[signature]*

School Report - Age 11 - NO CHANGE

| me | Ian Griffiths | Form | 1A3 | ATTAIN | C |
| ject | English | Set | | EFFORT | C |

Ian makes up in personality what he does not give to his written work. He has original ideas and a sense of humour but is too slap-happy.

133

CENTRE PAGE FEATURE - "BLUE JEANS" MAGAZINE

134

King Of Comedy

Sunday evenings, renowned for being singularly unamusing, are about to get a whole lot funnier as a new monthly comedy evening launches at Bar R. Main man Griff Griffiths fills us in...

It's twenty past six on a Monday morning and I've just woken up, fully clothed (still with coat on) sitting bolt upright on my sofa. The tv volume is turned up to 11 and 'The Hoobs' are having an argument over which of Groove's collections to throw away as they're too heavy and the Hoobmobile won't go. The Motorettes are, apparently, knackered. I know how they feel. Had today's question for Hoob News been something such as, 'How did the Editor actually get home last night' that would have been helpful, as I haven't got a bloody clue...

Jump back exactly twelve hours then, and I'm sat in the Porter and Sorter waiting for one Griff Griffiths, comedian and orchestrator of a new Sunday night comedy evening at Bar R (or Rendezvous, for the old skool massive). I reckon I know what a comedian looks like and am glancing around the pub, ma-hus-ive glass of Merlot in hand, looking for a skinny student type, probably wearing ironic trousers. What I'm not looking for and, as it transpires, should be, is a bloke built like a brick shit-house who looks somewhat like Ray Winstone, for this is Mr Griffiths.

'What's the best heckle you've ever had?' I say, thinking that no-one in their right mind would dare.

'It wasn't so much a heckle, but I played a gig for some social workers in Summerstown, near King's Cross, and the regulars weren't happy. I was on stage for 6 seconds when this bloke shouts 'You're fucking shit', so I say, jokingly, 'you what mate?' and he walks all the way to the stage, gets up, takes the mic and says 'You're fucking shit'. I got my coat...'

As ever, appearances can be deceptive, as it turns out Griff is probably one of the nicest blokes you'd ever hope to meet, although possibly not by surprise in a dark alley, he is also, as well as being a chirpy saarf london geezer, a Romany Gipsy. His mum is the 7th daughter of a 7th daughter, which apparently makes her a witch, whereas Griff believes 'his dad (a small bloke) is the 7th son of the 7th son of one of the 7 dwarves'. He is also, today, hungover, having just come back from a gig in Bristol, one of over 260 he's played since turning to comedy just 18 months ago, after previously being a

drummer for 12 years (he had his own fan club and appeared in Smash Hits, My Guy, Blue Jeans and Just 17, amongst other mags) and a furniture magnate. So what prompted this radical change of career?

'A nervous breakdown, to be honest. I was in The Priory for a while, where I thought I was the King of Spain. Apparently that's quite a common thing. You never get people in there thinking they're a plumber or electrician or something, it's always something quite grand, and I was the King of Spain. I can't even speak Spanish!

'I've had quite an interesting life, and what with the King of Spain thing, I thought it would make good comedy, which it turns out it does - it's been going really well, and it's opened a load of doors to different things. Someone came to see me at a gig and offered me a part in the new Hard-Fi video, for 'Cash-point'. I

'I'm in the new Hard-Fi video playing a copper. I was quite convincing, I even moved a couple of fly-tippers on...'

play a miner and a copper, with all the gear. I was quite convincing, oddly. I even went and had a policemanly word with a couple of fly-tippers over the road! It's out 5th December, so keep your eyes peeled for me.'

Frankly mate, we could hardly miss you, but this new-found jet-set lifestyle is still quite a change from owning a furniture business or sitting behind a drumkit for a living, and I'm intrigued to find out how you actually start being a comedian.

'I started doing open mic slots of 3 minutes and I just went from there. Now I'm getting paid for it! It's terrifying though, to start with. If you're a drummer, you're behind everyone else so 3 minutes, although it doesn't sound like a lot, is a long time to be on stage on your own with just a microphone.'

I actually know this to be true, although without the stage and microphone bit as, as regular readers of this magazine will know, I once subjected myself to a horrendous evening of speed

dating, in the name of investigative journalism, where each date lasts just 3 minutes but seems to go on for an eternity, and that's not even with an audience (except the unfortunate date-ee). At least you don't get people coming up to you and saying you're shit while you're doing it though, unless you really do need to brush up on your social and inter-personal skills.

But back to the night in question, a new and shiny comedy evening on the second Sunday of every month where six acts, including a compere, will make you laugh on the day before you go back to work, all for the entrance price of a measly quid and from the pulpit-like environs of the Bar R stage. The aims of the night are clear, as Griff explains;

'We want it to be a social thing, not rows of people staring at a comic on stage, more relaxed, with no pressure, and for it just to be more of a fun evening out. It's something different for a Sunday. I'm headlining the first one and we've got Dave Ward as a compere, and a guy called Imran Yusuf, who's very funny, and does a brilliant impersonation of a velociraptor, bizarrely. We'll also have open mic slots for anyone who wants to have a go at being funny.'

But, be warned, people, as everyone knows, it's one thing to be funny down the pub in front of your mates, and another thing entirely to make a room full of strangers laugh, so be prepared.

'It is frightening. I still get nervous before a gig - if I didn't, it'd be time to do something else for a living. I'm generally terrified before I get the first laugh, which is usually after my first joke, which is handy! But I enjoy what I do. The play, being a comedian, isn't that great, but I love what I do now. It beats working for a living! I'd encourage people to give it a go, it's a great job...'

So there you have it, if you want to have a fun evening out laughing with the erstwhile King of Spain, or scare the bejeezus out of yourself by actually having a go, it looks like the second Sunday of every month is going to be booked up, in our diaries at least, for the foreseeable future. Olé!

'Griff's' Comedy Night at Bar R kicks off on Sunday November 13 at 8pm (first act 8.45pm), and every second Sunday of the month thereafter. £5 entrance

My "Mohican" Stock Car Prior to knocking out Philip Schofield at the race
at Wimbledon

NO:	0000000000	PERIOD ENDED
BALANCE (£)		
340693.83−		
340577.75−		ELECTRA S
340601.82−		2 QTR 89
340335.59−		3 QTR 88

"Never to be paid" Bill after leaving ARISTA RECORDS - a great deal of
wedge in 1987, infact a great deal now

THE FOUR DOCTORS

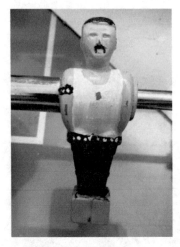

FREDDIE MERCURY

SPIDER MAN

CAPTAIN SENSIBLE

KIM JONG UN

RONNIE KRAY   KEITH MOON

HARRY POTTER   GHANDI

DALAI LAMA

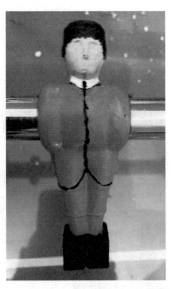

JOHN LENNON

I love this - Dee Dee Ramone. Created during one of my "ARTISTIC" periods. Look at the guitars on the flag can't really remember painting it!!

The "GRIFF" identity bracelet found amongst the remains at a school
caretakers destroyed pampus grass

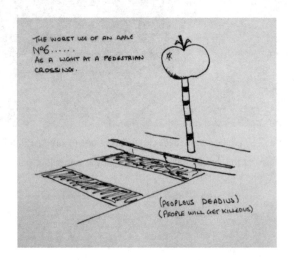

A SECTION OF THE BAYEUX TAPESTRY, DEPICTING NORMAN KNIGHTS RELAXING AFTER THE BATTLE.

(NOTE.... NORMAN KNIGHT TO LEFT OF ILLUSTRATION CARRYING SOME KIND OF WOMANS HANDBAG)

(HAVING FUNIVS AFTER KILLINGVS)

A BIRDS NEST WITH A FIRE ESCAPE.

(BIRDUS ESCAPEUS BLAZUS)

TO STRENGTH

The GREAT NUMBER ONE TEASE

Meet **Strength**, two new chaps who can break our hearts any day, especially when they put out such good stuff as 'Breaking Hearts'.

But far from breaking your hearts, Billy and Griff (the boys in the band) plan to make your day — they want to whisk one lucky winner off to a posh London health club where you can have a dip in the pool, work out on some weights, steam in the sauna and get kitted out in a brand new track suit and trainers all for now!!

So if that tickles your funny bones and you're just dying to get fit for the summer, then just tell us how many tons did Jonathan King have, plus a feather?!?

Answers on a postcard to Strength/Number One, 28th Floor, King's Reach Tower, Stamford Street, London SE1 9LS.

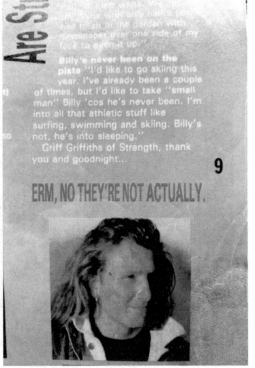

... ... which we ... ... with only half a ... ... to sit in the garden with ... newspaper over one side of my face to even it up."

Billy's never been on the piste "I'd like to go skiing this year. I've already been a couple of times, but I'd like to take "small man" Billy 'cos he's never been. I'm into all that athletic stuff like surfing, swimming and skiing. Billy's not, he's into sleeping."

Griff Griffiths of Strength, thank you and goodnight...

9

ERM, NO THEY'RE NOT ACTUALLY.

146

WITH ALAN BOWN IN NEW ORLEANS

WITH ALAN HANSON IN BENIDORM

'60s music legend, ALAN BOWN, was once my manager.

Wrote and produced a 'Summer' single; THE FLOB A **LOB** RAP, with a good friend Roger Murray. Had two fat blokes dressed as Bill and Ben, T-shirts saying "You're Ard Intcha" as a tribute to Frankie says "RELAX" printed. First photo shoot in Kew Gardens — I knew it was doomed to fail as the 'two fat DJs' Paul and Steve both suffered hay hever! We had a laugh though.

I draw cartoons and paint.

Euro 2017 with loads of Palace fans off to Europe to see football. Massive violence erupted, planes of Russian ex special forces were flown in to 'beat up' English fans. We decided not to go, we can all have a row but we aren't Power Rangers. My mate Ginge put a pin in a map and off we went to Spain, where I met my wife. At first, I thought she was Spanish, but she was just pissed.

Local pub, The Stag and Hounds, played a massive part in my life, and the lives of my older brother and social group. A big Victorian boozer where I was a regular from aged thirteen. It was the site of numerous fights, sexual encounters, drug deals, products of doubtful origins, etc. Every misdemeanour and moody scene one can imagine was played out in The Stag. A whole chapter could be dedicated to that magical place.

The night before Firework night when I was fourteen, we were drinking in the Stag.

Pissed, on the way home I was hit by a car. I went through the windscreen, bounced off the front seat and was hit a second time by the same fucking car.

A major accident. Mum and dad pleaded with the doctors not to amputate my mangled arm. I missed six months of school and used to Sellotape a drumstick into my hand so I could drum. Still have issues with it to this day.

When the pub was being demolished, I climbed the scaffolding and 'liberated' the Stag and Hounds sign… which is now pride of place on my shed.

Had two company vans — one a tiny Bedford Rascal. My salesman and close mate, Jocky, used it Friday afternoon. He picks me up from my house in Sutton, driving for early Friday beers. Suddenly he shouts "No," and we run a cat over. He wasn't going to stop but I made him. There in the gutter is a half-squashed cat! Not a cat fan but we've run it over. My first thought was to kill it. Then some young girl shouts "Tiddles, Tiddles." She runs over in hysterics. She hasn't got a motor so we decide to take her and the cat to a vet… she's in the back devastated, the cats in a box, Jocky wants to get to the pub… Anyway, drops her to the vet and off we go. We spoke about what's just happened over a pint, then it's history.

A couple of months later, new neighbours move in. An invite was received through the door for a housewarming with apologies for the noise that their housewarming party may cause. My wife's in bed, I'm lying on the second floor in darkness watching the people coming and going next door. Some familiar-looking tart wanders out and calls out "Tiddles, Tiddles," and from the darkness a fucked up, crippled cat drags itself across the lawn. What are the odds of firstly, the cat surviving being squashed by my van, then becoming my new neighbour?

They quickly moved away but before leaving, they stabbed all my tyres, broke my aerial… would have been cheaper to pick up the vet bill. Proof cats have nine lives!

Freemason — a member of a secret society dedicated to mutual help, brotherly love and fellowship. At the time of writing this I am The Worshipful Master of my Masonic Lodge — Lodge of Resolve No. 7177 — I have been a mason for over ten years. My dad joined at the age of twenty-two. He is now eighty-five. My uncles and cousins and brother are all Masons. My grandad started his own Lodge, so becoming a mason was inevitable.

Lots of ancient rituals, lots of study, tons of dedication is needed if one desires to climb the Masonic ladder. Google 'Freemasons' and our 'secrets' will be revealed with one click of a button. Like any 'hobby' you get out of it what you put in. Apparently, we are working with 'THE ILLUMINATI' to control the world. From my ten years' experience as a Mason, I know for a fact it's a nightmare organising a charity golf event with an evening BBQ. Clearly, it's an impossible leap from arranging a golf day piss up to secretly controlling the free world's finances as allies of 'The Illuminati'. It takes nearly a month for most of my Masonic mates to respond to an e-mail.

I have met and become very close, lifelong mates, with many characters that I would never have met or have anything to do with if not for our joint involvement with the Masons. A force for good.

I dated a beautiful girl who was a couple of years younger than me. She lived just around the comer. I was eighteen, she was sixteen. As usual, her parents hated me.

One night she came to a family function, we had sex on top of a grand piano. We dropped her home in my dad's Rolls later than her parents expected. Dad was pissed so mum was driving. Alison, my brother Nick and his future wife, Sarah, in the back. As we pulled into her driveway her mum and dad flew out, disgusted at how late she had arrived home. In reality I reckon they didn't like our happiness, hated their dull lives and both needed a bloody good shag. Our relationship ended. For at least eight years I would anonymously send roses and a card every Valentine's Day.

Fast forward a few years... I'm in LA with our American A&R man downtown, scoring drugs from some DJ in a moody club, turn round and directly behind me is Alison! It has to be fate. She was looking hot and I have to say, so was I. Turns out she's now a long-haul stewardess for BA, staying in LA for three or four nights. We exchange numbers and arrange a night out. I'm totally convinced we were destined to be as one! Level 42 were on tour and playing in town the next night. I get two tickets and backstage guest passes, arrange a limo, contact Alison and going to pick her up from her hotel the next day.

Arrive at hotel and she isn't in reception so I get the desk to call her room and she tells me that she isn't joining me and is going out with the pilot and crew that night. She didn't even come down and meet me! I was devastated. I went to the gig alone.

It transpires that the eight years I sent Valentine flowers they were never received because they sold the house nine years previously. I can only imagine the kind of aggravation and accusations that happened between the new couple that lived there when twenty red roses and a card saying "I'll never forget you" signed "you know who I am" arrived at the door every Valentine's Day.

Strangely I still believe in fate — with a few exceptions.

I was charged with criminal damage at Tooley Street Court after being caught graffitiing on a school for the blind directly opposite a police station — should have planned that better!

I'm fifty-eight and the only meal I've properly cooked is 'wild mushroom risotto' from a recipe in a Gary Rhodes cookbook my brother gave me as a Christmas gift.

My family home was built in 1858 for the Lord Mayor of Croydon — Ramacre Cottage. Of all the places I've visited and numerous houses I've lived in, Ramacre is the only place I've truly felt safe and at home. I've never been in a house like it — totally unique: twenty-seven rooms (of varying sizes), four bathrooms, five bedrooms over three floors, staff wing with three bedrooms, tiny service stairs with closeable viewing window, main house with elegant staircase leading to three massive bedrooms. Two cellars, a sauna, all built around a 'grand entertaining hall' three floors high — eight doors to enter its own well and a genuine 'Scooby-Doo' secret passageway which opens by pushing a wall from the TV lounge, revealing a small corridor with access to a study. So many radiators they are fired by an 'industrial boiler'.

My German teacher, Mr Huns, hated me. Looking back, he probably hated everyone — teaching German in a shit comprehensive school on a rough council estate was his destiny.

Before each class he would fire a few questions at random pupils in German, stuff like "How many brothers do you have?", "Is it raining today?", "What car does your dad drive?" He hated me because I said, "Dad drives a Rolls Royce," — not my fault. Anyway, at about age eleven I've moved into Ramacre. He asks me "Griffiths, how many rooms in your house?" I said, "I don't know, sir, maybe thirty," In English he shouts "Thirty! You idiot. Moron. Get out. You're the only person I've ever taught who can't remember the place where they live." He did have a point I suppose because there's only twenty-seven rooms. Ironically my son now lives in Munich and speaks German fluently. I think he has seven rooms in his apartment, though I've never asked.

I possess a certain amount of artistic ability and creative flare that pops its head up with no warning. During a two-week period, I can make stuff with very little effort, painting maybe ten images in an evening. Once that 'need to create' fades, I have absolutely no interest to paint at all. In fact, most of the images I've finished during those busy days I've got no idea how I did them. That's my excuse for only painting a third of the exterior of my house which I started nine years ago.

With thirty Crystal Palace fans, I went to Benidorm to celebrate a mate's birthday and catch three England games while there.

A brilliant picture was taken in a Spanish bar of us all enjoying pre-game drinks... on the telly behind us is Alan Hanson. The way the picture is taken it looks like he's on the piss with us.

Went out with a girl who was a qualified sports therapist. Our long-term plan was to buy a property in the Black Mountains, Wales. She would keep horses, I would have numerous Rottweilers. I'd train as a therapist and together we would treat walkers etc. at our own private clinic.

I never really studied at school but to gain the qualifications needed I had to attend evening and weekend classes at The London School of Massage based in Regents Park, London. Two years later, I passed the exams even though the day before I sat them, my older brother passed away!

Our relationship ran out of gas so the plans of owning a farm in the middle of nowhere didn't happen. I did run a clinic from my house for a few months and was gradually building a strong client base. We split up and I never practised again.

In 1997 I won the lottery twice in the same year, both times while on holiday — £23,000.00 when skiing in Saas-Fee, Switzerland, and £5,000.00 while enjoying the sun in Kefalonia, Greece. Seems to me like I should always be on holiday.

Held a 'mad hat' party — everybody had to come wearing crazy head regalia and there was a prize for first place. There were some excellent handmade hats. I had a model of D-day landings. There was an enormous fish, an iron, a mobile phone. Everyone made the effort. My mate Gary Powell (stunt man) turns up wearing a model of The White House on his head and floating above it on a wire was a spaceship... his entry was 'Independence Day'.

Judges decided a musical hat won first prize till Gary says, "Watch this coz you may change your decision..." He stood on the winner's podium, pressed a button and his whole head burst into explosions and flames for about eight minutes while he stood perfectly still. Expected from a Hollywood stuntman specialising in pyrotechnics.

1987, Los Angeles, there was a roar in our hotel. Noise and rumbling, as if an enormous delivery truck was manoeuvring in the apartment below. When the bed and furniture started to move, it was time to leg it. Obviously, every other resident had the same idea as we gathered, en masse, around the swimming pool where the water was splashing out in crashes similar to an over-excited wave machine at a local leisure centre.

I was experiencing California's most destructive earthquake for eighty years. A completely overwhelming feeling of total helplessness, as there was nowhere to run.

Two or three days later, I've flown back to the UK. The night I land, England suffers the violent hurricane — 15 or 16 October 1987.

Thought maybe I was in some way responsible, like an apocalyptic horseman, or a demon Antichrist. I was kind of waiting for a plague of locusts or terrible floods to strike South Croydon. Turns out I possess no such powers of destruction.

A few good mates of mine were in the military — ex marines and ex paras. They now run a successful military fitness boot camp in Norfolk. I've been there many times when feeling fat and unfit, and always come away from my two weeks stay there feeling 100% and at least a stone lighter... probably because they force you to go run about all day long and feed you fuck all. Anyway, on my way to one of my self-inflicted starvation stays there, I find myself ahead of schedule so I decide to visit The Military Museum at Duxford. As well as a museum it's an active airfield where they specialise in restoring, maintaining and flying old military aircraft.

After roaming about for a while, I find myself on my own, sitting on a bench, with a coffee and a bacon roll, watching a biplane about to land. It lands two hundred yards away, then slowly taxis and stops approximately 10 feet from where I'm sitting. Jokingly I say to the pilot "Gis a go!" He says, "Come on then." Before I had time to reconsider, I've put down my breakfast, donned a flying helmet and I'm in the open cockpit, behind the controls of a vintage Tiger Moth.

I've flown small aircraft many times but the experience of vintage flight in a plane that's older than the joint ages of my parents, made entirely from washing line parts was truly exhilarating.

After a few basic stunts we landed — my coffee was still warm and my bacon roll was waiting. Never even knew the pilot's name.

If he'd said, "OK, come back in half an hour," I probably wouldn't have gone. IF YOU DON'T ASK YOU DON'T GET.

One night after the pub I decided to have a BBQ in my flat —
wasn't such a good idea according to the neighbours, the
police and the fire brigade. Won't be seeing 'The Indoor BBQ'
on the next episode of Dragons' Den.

My older brother was a very successful noise in the city. He travelled the world, was a Freeman of the City of London (he can walk his sheep over London Bridge), friend of Princess Anne, Nelson Mandela amongst others. His house was so big you could hide five fat blokes in his garden and not find them.

He played water polo for England School Boys, swam for Surrey, an exceptional rugby player and sportsman. He retired at thirty-eight and drank himself to death.

Worked at Rock City Studios, Shepperton — Gary Numan's studios. Well-known at the time — he was so embarrassed about his lack of hair, however his biscuit tin only contained 'garibaldis'.

Two Benedictine monks took a lifelong vow of silence. They were sitting on the top deck of a bus and witness a terrible fatal car crash. One monk turned to the other monk and didn't say a fucking word.

Spent three hours looking for love on "plenty of fish" website till I realised it was an angling club in Kent?

Dressed as a vicar when I went to pick up my son at Gatwick
airport — no idea why!

I was a member of the British Carriage driving team — not ever an ambition of mine, in fact I had never heard of it, it was the hobby of my girlfriend at the time. Up till then the closest I had been to a horse was at a football match. Every other weekend during the summer we were up and down the country competing. Generally, horse people only like other horse people. They knew immediately I was not one of them. Accent, speech, attire, listening to Saturday football results — just four things that gave me away.

Anyway, every year a major weekend event is held in grounds of Sandringham. This is where I met Prince Phillip. He never missed the event, was always a time steward, pissed, and at the evening functions would touch up all the women — so met him on a few occasions. All the Royal Family are much smaller than one would imagine.

Didn't want my son to have the education I had, so both me and my ex-wife worked hard to put him through private education, from nursery, infants, senior school, college and university. Brilliant move, but he speaks like Boris Johnson.

For approximately a two-year period, every time I went shopping, I would secretly drop a flan base, into the shopping basket of a complete stranger. No one needs a flan base. They would have no idea of their purchase till packing their bags.

My Dad - I wouldn't mess with him!!

Mum & Dad at their wedding -1956

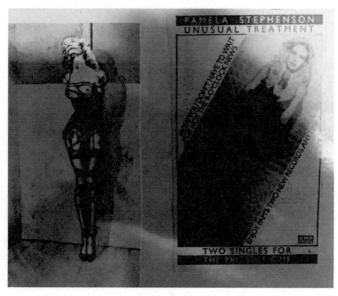

The Bad Actors single design
Stolen by Pamela Stephenson

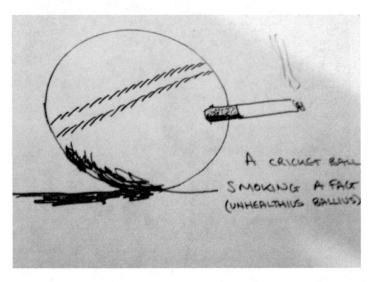

A CRICKET BALL
SMOKING A FAG
(UNHEALTHIUS BALLIUS)

A WHALE WITH A QUIFF
(MAMMALUS ELVICIS)

My disguise to gate crash Pink Floyds Party

I was at some weekend convention in Gibraltar, I think, or possibly Malta. Wall-to-wall musicians. I was walking down this curved marble staircase in reception when the model who fronted the single Ride on Time, Black Box, pulled my pony tail saying "Ding-dong". I turn and there's Rick Astley — "Ding-dong, you cunt," pushing him in the chest. To be honest, I did not expect much of a response but he wanted it, punching me on the side of the head.

Amazed he wasn't a dwarf, amazed he wanted it and let's be fair, I'm not a fan but no one expects confrontation with Rick Astley. We rolled downstairs, no one getting on top, me thinking I can't let Astley get the better of me. At the bottom of the stairs, we were pulled apart by none other than two or three members of Aswad. Off he went shouting that I was a wanker, off I went seriously asking myself if that really happened. My wife and me heard his radio show twenty-five years later, she said I should phone in to see if he remembers, but I couldn't take the rejection if he didn't.

On my own, mountain biking in Cornwall. I cycled from St Ives along the coast to Portlethen, then across the boot of England to Falmouth. Knackered and covered in shit — really busy, people everywhere, all roads cut off by barriers — I pushed my way in to see what was going on. Directly in front of me was Camilla Parker Bowles. Being big, bald headed, covered in shit, wearing a high-vis, she immediately shook my hand asking what I had been doing. "Cycling," I said. We shook hands and I could see her saying to herself "Oh dear, this peasant is covered in shit." Fate. Some people had been waiting half the day to see her — I had been there eight minutes. Personally, going on looks alone, I think Charles chose poorly.

I was recording an album in Toluca Lake at a studio owned by Frank Sinatra Junior. Saw Frank Sinatra Junior one day, in he comes with his dog... I went to stroke the dog and it bit me. I said "You could have told me your dog bites," to which he said "Let me tell you, man, everything with a mouth, bites."

The dog bit me his way.

Royalty

I met the Queen with my mum and older brother on a walkabout in Wandsworth in 1977.

I became friends with World War Two legend Ulrich Steinhilper after meeting him at Biggin Hill Air Fair where I invited him to join me in the VIP area. For many years I joined him annually at the air show. He was a Luftwaffe ME 109 pilot and Battle of Britain veteran who was shot down and captured. There aren't many people who can say they've got a WWII Messerschmitt Battle of Britain pilot's phone number on their contact list.

Living life to the full has made me really fat.

I was convinced that I wrote the novel Captain Corelli's Mandolin. I didn't really know what a mandolin was.

I'm not very good at certain things but really good at others.

I've had fifteen or sixteen singles released, two or three albums and appeared on many, many compilation albums — worldwide, in various bands.

One night, watching telly, suddenly had to paint. Painted my table football Crystal Palace versus Celebrity All Star 11 — all started and finished in one evening.

Celebrity All Star 11 included:

- In goal: Harry Potter
- Defence: Dalai Lama - Ghandi
- Midfield: Spider-Man – Rupert the Bear - John Lennon - Ronnie Kray
- Upfront: Captain Sensible - Kim Jong-Un - Keith Moon – The Hulk

- Did have Darth Vader on the wing but he was only on loan.
- Bloody dream team.

My grandad owned all the fields which now house HEATHROW AIRPORT. They were compulsory purchased from him for a pittance. LEGAL ROBBERY!

Uri Geller is a fake spoon-bending mother fucker, and if he came round to my house messing with my cutlery, fucking about with my knives and forks, and destroying the contents of my cooking utensil cabinet, I'd kick his fucking head in.

Mind you, he hasn't been round so maybe he "can" read my mind!

Every member of a boy band is a dwarf.

My uncle John and his wife, my auntie Daphne, worked in the family business for my Dad. He was manager at a tyre yard in Richmond where two of my cousins also worked. He lived in a big place above another of Dad's premises in Tooting — a stone's throw from Tooting Broadway Station ('Power to the people', Citizen Smith). His daughter, my cousin Beverley, was eighteen and held her eighteenth birthday party in the flat over the shop. It was a big family do, also invited were loads of my mates —twenty or thirty maybe and another bunch of her mates from Tooting — twenty to thirty skinheads — obviously friction between two groups. Dad, plus a couple of uncles, intervened asking the skinheads to leave, which they did. One was not so compliant. I remember his name — Billy — never seen him before or since. Few words exchanged with my family and he started towards the stairs, walking past table with food, he sneakily picked up a knife (which I believed he was going to use on my dad). Without hesitation I knocked him out. I was jumped on by uncles who had no idea what I'd witnessed. Dad went crazy, not believing my account, and threw me down the stairs. On the way down I bashed a hole in the stairway with my head. In the car in silence, drove home — got home, mum phoned party to make sure all OK and some unrecognizable voice answered, screaming "Help, help, call the police," which we did.

The ejected skinheads had regrouped outside and attacked the party through doors, windows, up drainpipes, on the fitting bay roof — chanting in unison "Skinheads, Skinheads." From ground floor to first floor, second floor, with all mates defending by throwing furniture, plates, pictures down the stairs — like a scene from Zulu Rorke's Drift.

They stole all the party-goers coats etc., loads of stuff from the kitchen: toaster, plates, TV etc. They tried to get my pal Bod Lee out the door to give him a kicking, with my lot holding on to him by his arms. They actually nicked his shoes and broke both the DJ's arms!

To this day uncle John and auntie Daphne blame me. That night changed my parent's relationship with them forever — very rarely did we see them socially.

The fight was front page on the Evening News. They went to court on charges of affray but they all got off on a lesser charge.

Somehow, I ended up with a mobility scooter (no idea where it came from or why I happened upon it). I'd met a new girlfriend who was at my house, both pissed, we decided to take a trip to the twenty-four-hour Tesco, not too far from where I lived. We went through the woods and into the shop, both of us on the scooter — so pissed we were smashing into shelves and knocking stuff over. The manager said, "You can't use that in here."

I said, "I'm disabled."

He said, "No you ain't, I saw you walking about in the drinks aisle earlier."

To celebrate The Queens Jubilee in 1977, my school decided to plant a load of new trees at the main entrance. Next morning the whole school was called to an emergency assembly where we were told they had all been uprooted and stuffed down the boys' toilets.

I knew Charlie Kray (he wasn't my best mate by any standards). I first met him on a promo tour when he was promoting his book in a Stoke hotel. Since then, I've spent numerous nights on the piss with him in various pubs and nightclubs. I was running my own furniture company which included an art gallery with bespoke framing. At the time the Kray twins, Ronnie and Reggie, were creating their own style of artwork. I had the idea of trying to promote my business by framing their images with possible headlines like "Young entrepreneur frames the Kray twins". So I approached Charlie with the idea who put me in touch with their business adviser, Laurie O'Leary. After a couple of meets with him to discuss the next move, I decided it wasn't such a good idea after all… probably a good move because I wouldn't have been paid anyway.

Number One Magazine featured my band at the time, Strength, in a colour centre page spread, pictures, etc, kind of "a typical day in the life of us". They followed and photographed me from leaving my home, using the gym in the morning, working in the studio, relaxing playing table tennis, then photos at a live show that night.

I think maybe the week after, they ran some sort of promotion to coincide with the release of our latest record, where, if the six or so questions set out by the magazine were answered correctly, the first four lucky winners chosen could spend a whole day with me and the singer in a top London spa and health club, enjoying all the facilities, including: jacuzzi, swimming pool, sauna, hot tub, massage, etc.

The readership of Number One Magazine was predominantly girls — girls between the age of twelve and fifteen I should imagine.

I can't believe, even now, that this competition was an idea dreamt up by the press department at Number One Magazine.

I thought then it was an awful idea, a winning prize for four vulnerable teenage girls to wander around in swimwear with two blokes they fancy, from a band they dreamt about.

I refused to attend, under much duress, with nobody else really agreeing with me.

The winners were given alternative prizes; it's beyond question that these girls were in no danger if the spa day had gone ahead. I'm glad it didn't. I made a stand for what I truly believed was morally correct.

Looking back, I suppose it's an example of how life, society, our behaviour and what we believe to be acceptable today, is so different to what it was three decades ago.

The deep heat story.

After my divorce I would look after my son, Sam, every other weekend, and every Wednesday. He was still at school and at that time I was living at Caterham Barracks.

It's mid-winter and bloody cold. My house was a new build; four beds, four bathrooms.

Just as I was putting Sam to bed, the heating packed up — boiler stopped boiling. I had no back-up electric heaters and no idea whom to contact at such a late hour. The temperature inside dropped immediately. Sam was freezing. What should I do?

To this day I still think it's a genius idea. I decided the best way to warm him up was to spray him all over with Deep Heat. He was so hot that night that he slept on top of the duvet.

Unfortunately, the next day when he was asked by his mum if he had a good time at daddy's and what did you do, he told his mum that the boiler broke down and how cold he was... but not for long as daddy had a heat-generating, pain relief spray which he covered him in which warmed him up till morning.

There was a time when I would have been praised for such an action. I'm sure that if her current partner thought of that, he'd probably receive a gift of aftershave or some vouchers for Nando's. Back in the day she would have been proudly sharing that story at dinner parties to show what an outstanding husband I was. Not now.

All I got was a strongly worded letter and a text message from her best mate telling me to "grow up"!

My mum and dad lived in Blechynden Street, Notting Hill during the late 1950s when the race riots were happening. The place they once lived in has long gone, demolished to build the elevated dual carriageway section of the A40, known as The Westway.

This violent period in West London history is depicted in the 1986 film Absolute Beginners, starring David Bowie and Patsy Kensit.

I was working in Shepperton Studios where the film was being shot. During a lull in the recording session, myself and a good mate of mine, Mark Taylor (who was the keyboard player in The Alarm), wandered onto the film set. An entire London postcode, created out of fibreglass, exactly resembling the Notting Hill of 1958 when my mum and dad lived there.

I took loads of photos and showed them to my parents. We eventually got round to watching the film together. Mum, dad and I all agreed that they had definitely recreated the run-down, derelict, almost slum-like look of Notting Hill in 1958, but they both said the film was "shit".

Part of the coursework needed to qualify as a sports therapist, each candidate had to perform and document at least a hundred client massages — free or paid. Ideally bodies of all shapes and sizes, sex, age, etc. Normal people are easy to find. I gave myself a proper challenge by offering my palpation skills to my old mate, Big Roy.

Now, Big Roy is black, 6 feet 4 inches, built like the bloke with magical powers in The Green Mile. He was a passenger in a fatal car crash which left two of our pals dead and Big Roy in a coma for six months. He's permanently confused, can't feel pain, and laughs at anything humorous up to twenty-four hours after everybody else — however, a perfect challenging case study, guaranteed to impress any tutor. Cutting a long story short, eight to ten sessions later, working weekly on his sternocleidomastoid and levator scapulae (muscles in the neck), I'd achieved that much movement that he was able to tum his massive head so far round he could almost lick his own spine. He looked so unbelievable that I nearly entered him into that year's Britain's Got Talent.

Anyway, treatments over, no payment asked for, but Big Roy demanded I took some kind of reward for my time; I would drive to pick him up, then drive him home, always getting him an ice cream before dropping him off. Then, as he was getting out of the car, he said, "If you won't take money do you want me to hurt somebody, wipe somebody out for ya?"

I really appreciate the offer Roy, but nothing immediately springs to mind where the use of extreme violence is necessary. I'd rather you donate some money to a charity of your choice.

I wrote a whole comedy routine influenced by Big Roy about animals in my garden — even though I say it myself, it's a work of genius! I am still in touch with BIG Roy who lives in Bulgaria

The Eric Story. For many years I was very close to a good mate Eric. As we grew older our interests began to differ, and, like so many teenage buddies, we saw less and less of each other. Rarely see him now.

Maybe ten years ago, I was at his house where his front room was full of bags and bags of golf balls. He'd taught his dog to search and find 'em, then sold them on eBay, which is a business plan we won't be sending to Dragons' Den.

He's obsessed with metal detecting and found untold historic coins and small artefacts. One weekend he managed to persuade me and another mate, Paul the Carpet, to join him on an organised detecting event. Early in the morning we drove to a recently ploughed field in Norfolk, scores of detectorists turned up, all looking exactly the same, as if deriving from the same parents.

At the entrance to the field there was a 20 feet by 20 feet marquee, inhabited by four or five official historians — reason being if any finds of possible significance are found, they must be declared to the historians in case the area is a site of great historical interest or there are items worthy of display in a museum.

Anyway, after five hours I'm covered in shit, starving, freezing cold and soaked. My only two finds being a Capri-Sun packet and half a biro. In the distance Eric is waving, beckoning me over — he's found a 5-inch diameter, possibly brass, disc. He's convinced it's the boss (centre piece) of an Anglo-Saxon shield. He hides it in his rucksack because there's no way some official historian is nicking it off him. This was "the big one", his find of a lifetime, a discovery of untold wealth — he'd discovered a priceless piece of history that was going to change his life, making him rich and famous.